Fond Farewells

Stories That Comfort

When Saying Goodbye

By Rebecca Trowbridge

Art by Caitlin Bales

For Nigel, Zoe and Maya

www.fond-farewell.com

© Rebecca Trowbridge 2012. All rights reserved.

ISBN: 9781973520474

Awards:

Winner in the "Children's Picture Book: Softcover Fiction" category of the 2013 International Book Awards.

Finalist in the "Children's Mind/Body/Spirit" category of the 2013 International Book Awards.

Finalist in the "Childrens-Inspirational/Motivational" category of the 2013 National Indie Excellence Awards.

Also available:

Congraduations!

Cherry Chicken Chocolate Kitchen

Table of Contents

The Farewell

4

Oscar Moves Away

11

The Balloon Trip

24

This Long Goodbye

33

The Farewell

The Farewell

Our time together is ending too soon...

please don't forget me,

I know I'll miss you.

There's things I must do,

I must go far away,

so wish me farewell though I wish I could stay.

The Farewell

I'll put your gift where I'll see it each day

and hope that your travels are safe underway.

For though time and distance pull us apart,

special friends always live on in our hearts.

So until we see each other again,

I'll think of you well, and often, my friend.

Oscar Moves Away

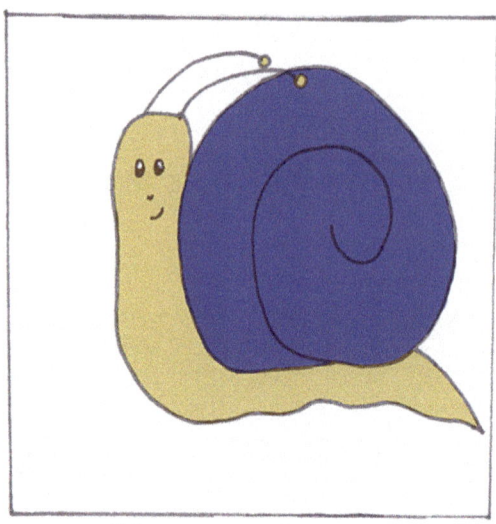

My name is Oscar.

I live in the woods.

I have fun with friends.

My life is so good!

But Mother and Father tell me some news:

we're moving on, to a beach lagoon.

I'm so unhappy.
I don't want to go.
It all looks so strange...
I feel so alone.

Sand and seashells and salt water too...

A pretty place, yet I feel so blue!

My parents enjoy a stroll and a swim;

I wish I was excited like them…

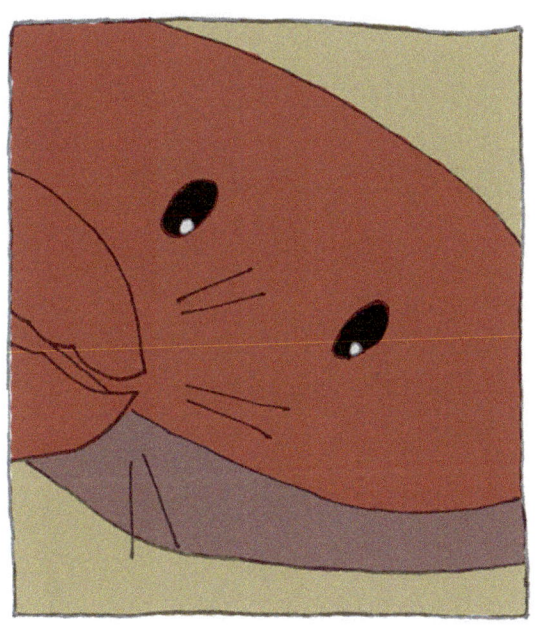

Then...SNAP!

Who's that!

Clickety clack!

And just like that, things aren't so bad.

Moving is scary,
but I'll wear a brave face.

Settling takes time—
I'll get used to this place!

So that means my old, hard shell needs to go!

I wonder what my friends would think,

'back home'?

Yes, we get to talk once in a while!
It makes me so happy
I just have to smile.

What a comfort that,

when change comes your way,

old friends are only

a phone call away!

The Balloon Trip

"It's all on the map! Adventure and glory!
I can't wait to start! It'll make a great story!"

Cat was excited, but also could see
Hedgehog was quiet with doubts and worries.

"I know you're concerned, but I'll be okay,
I'll keep you posted each step of the way."

"Farewell and good luck,"
Hedgehog graciously said,
"Try to stay warm...

The Balloon Trip

I'll miss you, old friend."

The Balloon Trip

Oh, so much to see!

Life's wonders abound!

The curious find

so much that astounds!

The Balloon Trip

And upon returning -

fair welcome indeed!

So much joy in the community!

But someone was missing in all of the din...

"Does anyone know if Hedgehog is in?"

And out of the crowd, reunited at last,

came a lesson about different life paths:

That after so long,

time apart is erased

in just a second,

by a friend's fond embrace.

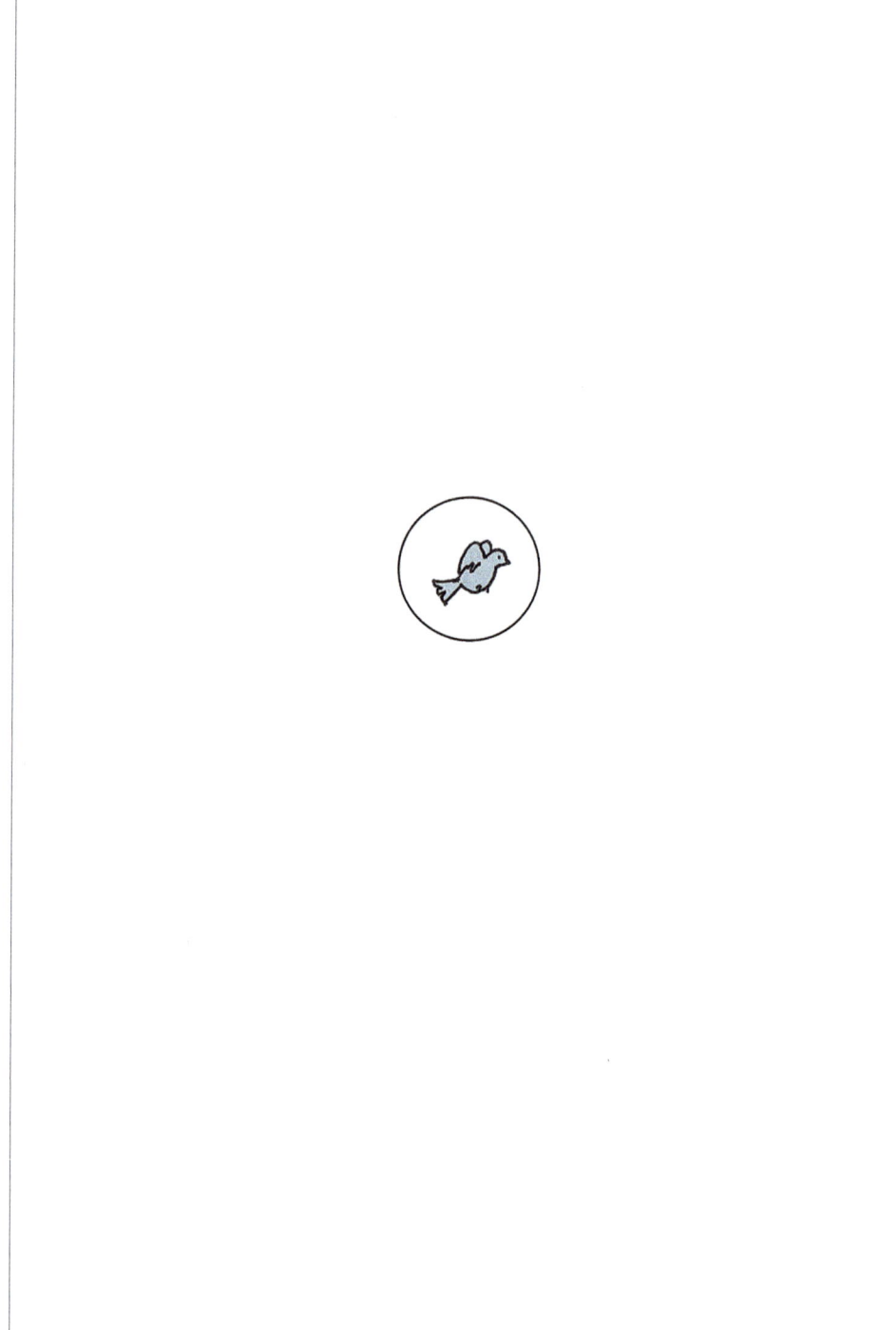

This Long Goodbye

Thank You for being here,

with me, one more time.

I know it's not easy:

this long goodbye.

When I depart,

it will be your kind face

that I see as I float

off... into space...

The trip will be lonely,

but I can be brave.

Because at the end,

a new family waits.

Please don't you worry, I'll feel right at home!

And though you'll miss me, you can let me go.

For one lovely day,

we will say hello.

Good-bye-ee!

(Robert Patrick Weston, 1917)

Good-bye-ee! Good-bye-ee!
Wipe the tear, baby dear, from your eye-ee!
Tho' 'tis hard to part, I know,
I'll be tickled to death to go.

Don't cry-ee! Don't sigh-ee!
There's a silver lining in the sky-ee!
Bonsoir, old thing! Cheerio! Chin-chin!
Nah-poo! Toodle-oo! Good-bye-ee!